RV Living for Beginners

- The Complete RV Camping Guide to Start Living the RV Lifestyle You've Been Dreaming About for Years •

By Kevin Masters

Disclaimer

Please note that the information contained within this document is for educational and entertainment purposes only. All effort has been executed to present accurate, up to date, and reliable, complete information. No warranties of any kind are declared or implied. Readers acknowledge that the author is not engaging in the rendering of legal, financial, medical or professional advice. The content within this book has been derived from various sources. Please consult a licensed professional before attempting any techniques outlined in this book.

By reading this document, the reader agrees that under no circumstances is the author responsible for any losses, direct or indirect, which are incurred as a result of the use of information contained within this document, including, but not limited to - errors, omissions, or inaccuracies.

Table of Contents

Introduction 5

Is This Just a Pipe Dream? 7

   The Pros 8

   The Cons 10

Getting Started: Making Your Plans 12

Choosing Your Ideal RV 15

   Types of RV 16

   Choosing the Right Fit 19

   Where to Buy From 24

Tips For Purchasing Your RV 25

   Tire Wear 26

   Get an Inspection 27

   Negotiate the Price 28

   Don't Worry Too Much 29

Spring Cleaning Your Life 30

An Anchor for the Anchorless 34

   Addresses 35

   Tax Benefits 36

   Vehicle Licensing and Registration 37

   REAL ID 39

   Health Insurance 40

   Banking 41

Jury Duty 42

Voting 43

Home Schooling 44

What About Your Pets? 46

RV Living On Your Own 50

Setting Up Your Budget 52

Firming Up Your Finances 58

Caring for your RV 62

Safety on the Road 65

Accidents 66

Safety Inside Your Vehicle 69

Safety From Wild Animals 70

Safety From Weather 73

Calling For Help 74

Choosing Where to Stop 77

Camping 78

Boondocking 80

Dispersed Camping 81

Short Stays 83

In Summary 85

Special Thanks 87

Introduction

To have itchy feet, a restless heart and a deep seated feeling of wanderlust is not strange, or wrong, or even something you'll never be able to fix. Not all of us are cut out for the same routine day in, day out, looking at the same faces and driving the same narrow streets.

For some of us, the nomadic ways of our ancient ancestors is still ingrained in our very DNA. We don't want to be stuck in the same office, climbing the same corporate ladder, cooking the same dinners and watching the same old tv shows.

We want to see what's around the next corner and over the next hill. We want the variety of never staying too long in one place – to explore, get to know and then move on.

There has never been a better time to give in to the desire that has niggled at you all along. You really can quit your job, get on the road in your RV and support yourself while seeing the country, discovering places you never knew existed and meeting people you'd never have come across.

In this book, we're going to prepare you to do exactly that, from preparing your vehicle to preparing yourself. Your adventure awaits you – all you need to do is let yourself make it happen.

Is This Just a Pipe Dream?

The simple answer to that question is: absolutely not. As long as you have the courage to forge ahead and the fortitude to learn everything you can about your new life before you embark, there's nowhere you cannot go.

The Pros

If you're wondering whether you will be able to afford this change, it might help to know that you're about to lower your costs considerably, and meanwhile you'll have very little trouble earning your crust as you travel. It might seem as though there ought to be a cost associated with a life of travel and adventure, but it's not going to be a financial one – RV living is incredibly low cost compared to renting a house or paying a mortgage.

If you're concerned that there's surely a reason more people don't do this, and that it can't be a good idea if there are so few nomads living in RVs across the country, there's more good news. What you're feeling is the natural human inclination to find safety – it's one of the core needs that we, as a species, feel compelled to satisfy, along with eating, drinking and sleeping.

Most people cannot break away from this need to build a stable core for themselves that will provide them with reliable shelter. Wanderlust is common, but not common enough to override this need for stability.

That doesn't make you wrong, it just makes you a little different to the norm. And it doesn't mean you can't make this work, because there's no basic need you can't satisfy from your life on the road. Not to mention that we humans are hugely adaptable to change – we just don't always think we are.

Really, the only thing you need to make this work is the determination to follow your dream. Close your eyes for a moment and think about what life will be like waking up in a different place every day, free from the normal constraints of routine and able to head in whatever direction takes your fancy.

No longer will you have to deal with the burden of maintaining and paying for a house. No more will you have to deal with the mountains of belongings that accumulate in it over the years. No longer will you be held back from doing the things you want to do because you're constantly being pulled back to the center of your world – your stationary, unmoving home.

From the moment you hit the road, you can go anywhere and do anything. As the old saying goes, the only limits will be your own imagination.

Does that appeal to you? Does it invoke feelings of excitement? Do you pine for that kind of excitement and find it appeals to you more strongly than any other lifestyle you can imagine? Then RV living might well be the choice for you.

The Cons

But on the other hand, it's best to be realistic. The romance of freedom is all well and good and you really will get to experience a way of life that makes you feel like a weight has lifted from your back and anything is possible. But you'll also be experiencing a lot of drawbacks. If any of these put you off, it might be best to think harder about your decision:

- You will need to put a lot of effort into maintenance to keep your home on the road, or you'll need to pay someone else to do it.

- You're not going to have a lot of living space, so this isn't an ideal lifestyle for the claustrophobic.

- Your income will not be lavish, so your spending cannot be lavish either. You will probably need to avoid shopping sprees and expensive meals.

- You are going to need to pare down your belongings to the barest minimum, with very little room for nostalgia.

- Your medical costs can be high if you have no home "network" for your insurance.

- You are going to spend most of your time away from everything that's familiar, including your friends and family and the environment you have been living in.

Getting Started: Making Your Plans

When you close the door of your RV, start the engine and hit the road, everything about your life is going to change – and we really do mean everything. That's why it's so important to prepare yourself and understand exactly what it is you want out of this adventure. There's a lot you're going to need to get done, and it's really going to help to know what goal you're trying to reach.

For instance, does RV living appeal to you because you have a desire to see as many places and sights as you possibly can? Is there a specific part of the country you want to spend time in but never had the chance?

Are you hoping to hit different places when events are going on that you always wanted to see, like festivals and concerts? Are you looking to follow Mother Nature and stick to places where the weather is good rather than slog through the snows of winter? Do you want to sleep out in the wilderness and escape from the confines of the city?

Everyone has a slightly different reason to seek the freedom of RV life, and that reason is going to influence your choices and actions in ways both small and large. You're about to get started on a long list of preparations and it's worth knowing your goals so that you can tackle them from a place of self understanding.

For instance, you're going to need to:

- Figure out your living budget so you know exactly how much you will need to earn to keep yourself comfortable and healthy while also partaking in the activities you are hoping to enjoy during your travels.

- Choose the right rig to fit your idea of comfortable nomadic living and that will be able to travel to the specific places you want to visit, over the type of terrain you hope to cover.

- Put together your kit of living materials, including all the items you will need to fit your new lifestyle.

- Decide what items you can get rid of or store before you leave, because your living space is about to shrink quite drastically.

- Work out how you will earn a living on the road and what you will need to take with you to make it happen.

- Figure out how, when and how much you want to make new friends and socialize with people on your travels.

- Decide where your home base will be – the place where you get your driver's license, are registered as a resident and can vote when the time comes. Obviously your choice will depend on convenience to your preferred area of travel.

This isn't a full list of the considerations ahead of you. There are also decisions to make on such things as whether to travel with pets, with whom to insure your belongings and how you will maintain your equipment. But what you can see from the list above is that your goals really will have an impact on your preparations.

So sit down right now with a piece of paper and write down all the reasons you have to embark on a nomadic lifestyle. Think hard about what you want to achieve, what you're looking to leave behind and where you want to go.

RV living gives you the freedom to be spontaneous and the power to choose your own path. But it's a lot easier to be spontaneous when you've diligently covered all your basic needs – and before you do anything else, to live the dream, you really do need to know exactly what the dream is.

Choosing Your Ideal RV

Your best friend and source of protection, comfort and safety in your new life is, of course, going to be your vehicle. It's a big decision and probably the one that's going to have the most influence on your future happiness, so it's also the first decision you should prepare yourself to make.

But a quick look at the internet is going to show you exactly what a hard decision this is likely to be. Unless you've started out with a specific RV already in mind, the choices can be seriously mind boggling.

There are simple caravans and state of the art motor homes, classes from A through C, converted vans and fifth wheels and everything in between. All these choices range in price from a couple of thousand dollars into the millions.

The types of rig available to you include:

- Class A – the largest available and the most luxurious, often with slide outs that increase the space available even more and very big holding tanks for water and waste. Many can also tow cars or boats. On the downside, they often have low gas mileage and can be hard to maneuver.
- Class B – these are usually under 23 feet and can be small enough to fit in a parking space. They have good gas mileage and are maneuverable and are subtle enough to be parked in the city streets.

- Class C – medium in size, these vary from 20 to 30 feet and usually have a bunk over the cab for sleeping. They usually have a bathroom and shower and sometimes have a slide out and some of the Class A luxuries. Most cannot tow a car or boat efficiently.

- Truck Campers – These are installed on the bed of a pick up truck and many have slide outs and over the cab bunks for space. They are great for moving around more rugged terrain and "pack down" to create a small profile for traveling, so they are often the choice of the RVer who wants to head to more remote places. They are, however, smaller in space and offer fewer amenities than other options.

- Fifth Wheel – These are the biggest style of trailer that can be towed by a truck and can reach up to 40 feet in length. They are hooked to the truck via a hitch mechanism, hence the name of "fifth wheel". This option can potentially be as luxurious as a Class A with the same number of amenities, such as slide outs and holding tanks, but they have the additional advantage of a separate vehicle that can be unhooked and used to move around while you are stationary. On the downside, you are going to need a truck with a significant towing capacity.

- Pop Up Trailer – These are attached to your truck via a bumper hitch and can be collapsed down while driving, popping back up to the size of a large tent. They don't have much in the way of amenities and they're not great in severe weather, but if you like the feeling of being closer to nature, they can offer you that without the need to sleep on the ground.

- Travel Trailer – There are a huge variety of travel trailers available, in a huge variety of sizes. They are pulled via a bumper hitch and your choice can be tailored according to the towing capacity of your truck. Again, these can be unhitched to allow you to use your vehicle around town while your home is parked up.

- Camper Vans – You can convert a camper van into a home that looks like any other van but really houses your home. It's great on city streets and for stealthily parking up at night, but you will have to put the time and effort in to convert it or pay for someone else to do it for you.

- Skoolies – This is the name given to buses that have been converted into homes, ranging from a school buses to the huge shuttle buses. Again, you'll need to strip and refit it yourself or pay for the work to be done, but the sky is pretty much the limit when it comes to choices. On the other hand, it's worth bearing in mind that many RV parks will not allow this kind of vehicle and your gas mileage probably won't be great. You'll also tend to stand out, so you won't have as much luck going incognito.

Choosing the Right Fit

Thanks to your thought exercise in the previous chapter, you do have somewhere to start. You have a fair idea of what you want to do and where you want to go, so you know the kinds of roads you'll be traveling and the necessities you won't be able to live without.

You'll have a list of must-haves in your head. For instance, you'll need holding tanks if you're planning to boondock (which means to RV without connecting to water, sewer and electric and also usually without having to pay a camping fee), you'll need plug-ins if you're thinking of doing freelance computer work to support yourself.

But you'll also probably have a few misconceptions, particularly when it comes to size. Most new RVers think they're going to need a much bigger rig than they will actually feel comfortable with, for example.

Unfortunately, there's one thing almost all veteran RVers will agree on and it's that you're really not going to be sure of your needs until you've been on the road for a while. All the careful thought in the world can't prepare you for the element of discovery that is exactly why you're doing this in the first place.

For instance, maybe you're absolutely sure right now that you have no interest in going off piste at night to sleep in the middle of nowhere. Once you get on the road and find yourself in a situation where you can give it a go, maybe you'll discover a love for that kind of living that you never expected to be the case.

Maybe you don't think you'll socialize much on the road, so you don't think you'll need much room in your living space, but then you discover you really enjoy inviting temporary work colleagues over for a beer and conversation.

The whole world is about to open up to you and it wouldn't be feasible to expect yourself to know what about it you'll love or dislike before you have a chance to experience it. Most RV veterans will advise you to choose as best you can right now but relax and aim for the affordable. In a year or two, you'll almost certainly be looking to exchange your first rig for one that matches your needs once you've had time to figure out what they are.

So let's start by writing a list of "must haves" for your first RV. You may not know what adventures are going to greet you, but you do have goals in mind to help guide you as you get started.

For instance, the size will be dependent on whether you are planning to travel to wide open spaces or narrow city streets. Good roads don't need rugged vehicles, but the back roads in the forests certainly do.

Consider your dietary needs – are you someone who likes to cook? What's your budget as you get started –do you need to avoid camping fees and will therefore need to hydrate and feed yourself and stay entertained without power or water?

How long do you plan to stay in each new place? If you're looking to stick around for a while and get to know each location, you won't need to worry about fuel consumption quite as much as if you're aiming to travel almost every day.

Take your time on this list – it's important. Try to include everything you think will be a priority for your own preferences and to achieve your personal dream of life on the road.

Once you have this list in hand, you can start your search. At this point, you'll start to discover another important fact about RV life: everything is a trade off.

To have one thing, you're likely going to need to give up something else. For instance, if you want to park up on a city street you'll need a smaller rig, but that's going to mean less living space. If, on the other hand, you want more living space, you're probably going to want to hook up a trailer to a vehicle instead of purchase an all-in-one RV, but that can be unwieldy or even impossible to maneuver on the back roads.

Towing also means you'll have a separate car or SUV to travel around town or sight see. But on the other hand, you can't simply get up and leave if you need to hook things up and unhook them – it's a lot more effort to get on the road.

If you intend to head for places with a lot of uphill terrain, you may want to consider a diesel engine. Again, there will be a trade off, because the power of your engine is going to be offset by the cost of buying and maintaining it.

Browsing the internet is not a great way to get to know the different options, because your choice is likely going to come down to what "feels" right. And to find something that "feels" right, you need to experience it first hand.

Find a local RV dealer and go for a visit. You are not looking to purchase right now, so leave your credit card at home if you're worried about impulse buying.

Wander through the selection and consider each one in turn. Look at how well it meets your personal needs and what you'll need to give up in return. Spend some serious time in the options that appeal to you – visit every room and think about what it would be like to live in that space.

What drawbacks does it have, and can you live with them? What benefits does it have, and are they the benefits you need? What's missing from your list, and is it something you can live without after all?

Price is, of course, also a huge consideration. Stick within your budget as you investigate. Once you have a fair idea of the kind of RV you're interested in, you can use the internet to find out what that model generally sells for. Try PPL Motorhomes to see a list of recent sales, or look at eBay and Facebook Marketplace.

Once you've whittled down your choices to a manageable few, it might help your final decision making to bear in mind that this is probably a vehicle you will want to sell in a couple of years. You want to be able to get your money back, or at least most of it, so condition is key and a bargain is absolutely the best option, even if it doesn't quite hit all the high points on your priority list.

Remember, you don't know exactly what your needs are going to be until you've got some experience under your belt, so don't sweat the small stuff quite yet. Go for the best bargain you can find with resale value, with your priority list coming in a close second. You will thank yourself later.

Where to Buy From

Once again, you're not going to be short on options at this point in the decision making process. You can find RV dealers pretty much anywhere in the country, so you'll have no issue finding a place to go look around. But you won't necessarily want to buy from one of these, as you may be able to get a better deal elsewhere.

Consider looking at RV Trader, an online platform open to both dealerships and private parties. RVT.com is another great choice, as is Craiglist and even Facebook. If you want to opt for a conversion, try Conversion Trader for a dedicated marketplace.

Tips For Purchasing Your RV

A few important considerations for the first time you purchase an RV, just to make sure you don't end up with a dud because you weren't aware of the risks. Whether you find a bargain for a few hundred dollars or spend out on the most luxurious RV you can find, there is always going to be the risk of something unexpected going wrong.

Tire Wear

First up, be absolutely sure to check the tires – and not in the same way you would check the tires on your vehicle. The treat on an RV's tires does not matter; what you are looking for is the age.

An RV tire is only good for between 5 and 7 years, because UV light and ozone cause them to deteriorate. "Dry rot", as it's known, causes cracks and will make a tire very dangerous to drive on.

Look for a four digit code on the tire itself – it may be on the inside, so you might have to get all the way underneath. That code is the week and year in which the tire was manufactured, so "1419" would be the fourteenth week of 2019.

Don't listen to your dealer if they point out there is plenty of tread on the tires and don't trust anyone else to do the checking for you. A tire blowout on an RV can be an extremely serious thing and your dealer may not be aware of the difference between tread and age.

Get an Inspection

As a beginner, it's unlikely you're going to know what to look for to be sure that your new home is in good condition. You may only be planning to keep it for a year or two before you trade it in, but you won't get a good price for something that has damage, mold and hidden problems.

Find an inspector through the National Recreational Vehicle Inspectors Association and hire them to take a thorough look at the RV you are planning to buy. This will cost you $500 or less and is worth every cent. If there's damage, you can avoid buying a dud or, at the very least, negotiate a much better price than the one you were expecting to pay.

Negotiate the Price

If you've done your homework and figured out how much your chosen vehicle usually sells for, you're already in a great position to negotiate a deal. Don't be afraid to negotiate and look for the absolute best price you can get – after all, this is the first step in building your new life and every dollar you save now is a dollar you can get back later and invest in your new vehicle.

Make a lower counter offer than you expect the seller to agree with and don't offer to split the difference – let them do that. Demand they do better and aim to get some extras thrown in to sweeten the deal, such as new tires or a thorough clean. Not everyone likes to negotiate, but it will be worth the effort in the end.

Don't Worry Too Much

It's natural to want to put as much effort as possible into this choice, but you really are going to look back at your diligent trudging of RV lots and all the fretting you did about styles and amenities and wonder why you bothered. There is no such thing as the ideal RV and you're not going to pick the ideal RV for you the first time out – quite frankly, you don't have a clue what your ideal RV is going to be. So get a good deal, find something that works and make sure it's road worthy – that's all you need to worry about so you can get on the road and get this adventure started.

Spring Cleaning Your Life

You're about to pack up your life and redistribute it in a tiny vehicle that will be following you everywhere on your travels like the shell on the back of a tortoise. No matter how much you are drawn to that pared down style of living, it's not going to be an easy transition.

Even if you are already a minimalist, it's almost guaranteed that you're going to need to throw away a few things. For most of us, a lifetime of living in one place, perhaps interspersed with a few moves into different spacious buildings, is guaranteed to have led to the accumulation of a lot more stuff than you might realize.

Before you can embark, you are going to have to get rid of lot of those belongings. The more you get rid of, the happier you will be once you hit the road, but it's not going to feel that way while you're hard at work discarding pieces of your life.

It's ok to dread this part of it – after all, if you didn't need a thing, you wouldn't own it in the first place, right? But as you start sorting through all those drawers and cupboards, you're likely to find that you keep things for many more reasons than their being useful.

Some things we keep because we "might need them" some day, others we keep because we don't want the expense of replacing something we barely use. A lot of items will have emotional and sentimental value to you. Some will be gifts from important people in your life that you feel bad about throwing away.

If the discarding process is simply too much for you, don't forget you have options. You can rent a storage unit for the items you cannot bear to throw away but won't fit inside your vehicle. You can then come back later and check through your items – by the time you've been living the RV life for a year or so, you might well find that your attitude has changed.

Start this part of your journey early and take it slow – not just to minimize the distress of throwing things away, but also because it's not a small task by any means.

Start with the drawers and cupboards you rarely open. Those contain the things you're least likely to need in your RV, and also the things you're least likely to miss if you throw them away. You can make a big dent in your project pretty quickly that way, which will be a fulfilling way to inspire yourself to keep going.

Unless it's clearly something that can go, don't throw things away immediately. Clear a big space and start three piles: one for the things you are absolutely sure you will keep, one for the things you would like to keep hold of and one for the things that need to go.

Once everything is in its pile, you can go through each one in turn. The pile of items you would like to keep probably contains quite a lot of duplicated items, particularly when it comes to clothing, so you will probably find some items you can move to the pile of things that need to go.

When you look at your pile of items that will be coming with you, you can now see where there are gaps that need to be filled. You may be able to move a few items from the second pile over to fill these gaps – if not, these are necessities you'll need to secure before you set off.

As for the pile of items that can go, don't throw them in the trash just yet. Anything that is in good condition can be sold via a yard sale, word of mouth, Facebook or even eBay. You could make a nice nest egg for yourself as you prepare to leave by doing this. Collectible items in particular could net you a nice wad of extra cash for emergencies and unexpected expenses.

You could also gift some of your items to friends and family, especially if they have sentimental value. This could alleviate the guilt or worry about throwing them away, while still allowing you to pare things down to the appropriate levels.

Once you've sold or thrown away the discard pile, kitted out your RV and probably snuck a few things from the second pile into spare spaces, you should be left with just one pile: the things you want to keep but don't have any room for in your vehicle.

At this point, you have a choice. You can either throw away and sell these items or choose to store them in a rental unit. Find out how much it would cost for a unit that will store everything you have left over – is it a worthwhile amount? Can you justify the cost in your new, lower cost lifestyle?

You may be lucky enough to have friends or family who will keep a box or two of special items for you – if so, can you pare down that pile to an appropriate level? If you do decide to keep some items in a rental unit or with loved ones, plan to come back after a year and revisit them to see if you really do want to keep them after all.

And that's it – your life now fits into a small RV and can come with you everywhere you go. It was a painful process, for sure, but don't you already feel that weight lifting and a feeling of freedom settling on your shoulders instead?

An Anchor for the Anchorless

The whole point of transferring your life into a home that has wheels and can go anywhere is that you no longer need to be tethered to a single point. On the other hand, you are still going to need to choose a permanent home, at least in terms of what state you are considered a resident of.

It doesn't have to be the state in which you were living before you hit the road – it doesn't even need to be a state you've ever visited. You can choose any you like, and you'll find that each one has a different set of potential drawbacks and benefits.

It's going to take some research to figure out the right one for you, and you may want to consult a CPA along the way to be sure that the tax situation will be right for you. The three most popular choices for RVers are South Dakota, Florida and Texas, because these states make it particularly easy for you to establish a domicile and keep it maintained; they also have no state income tax.

So why do you need a home state? Lots of reasons, from paying your taxes and opening bank accounts to voting during the elections. Let's take a quick look at each of them to help you decide which state will be the right choice for you:

Addresses

You need a physical and mailing address. The first is where you live, the second is where your mail is sent. A legal address for residency in a state must always be a street address – a PO Box usually won't suffice. However, if the state you choose provides easy access to mail forwarding services, this will give you the street address and is usually quite easy to do.

Tax Benefits

This is a big one, because it will have a huge impact on your finances along the way. Some states do not have their own income tax, so they are obviously not going to remove any dollars from your hard earned pay check. These states include: Alaska, Florida, Nevada, South Dakota, Texas, Washington and Wyoming. New Hampshire and Tennessee are also possibilities as they only tax the income on interest and dividends.

It's also worth noting that some states do not have sales tax (though they may have other local equivalents throughout the state). These are: Delaware, New Hampshire, Oregon, Alaska and Montana.

It's also worth looking into additional potential tax benefits. For example, some do not tax your Social Security income and others do not tax pensions. Depending on your personal circumstances, these can be very lucrative benefits.

Vehicle Licensing and Registration

You can't live in a vehicle without having a license to drive it and a registration to make it legal, and these are things you are going to need to obtain from your chosen home state.

They are also things you will need to obtain in person and need to be periodically renewed, so it's not a great idea to choose a home state that isn't going to be anywhere near your planned area of travel. For instance, if you're going to spend most of your time in the South and you don't have a passport to travel through Canada, it's not going to be easy to pop over to Alaska to get your documentation sorted.

On the other hand, some states will allow you to renew your documents online, so that's worth checking into before you make your decision. Some will require you to obtain them in person the first time and will then allow you to visit their website when it's time for renewal.

An additional consideration is that each state sets its own time periods for renewal. In some, it could be four or five years; in others, it might be eight. The longer the better if you aren't planning to stick close to your home state.

You should also look into whether or not the state you are considering requires safety inspections and emissions testing. Some will require you do these things annually, which is another binding factor you might not want to deal with.

Some states will also require special licenses for certain types of vehicle, which can take a while to process, while auto insurance is going to vary from place to place. Your insurance is based on the likelihood of needing a payout, so if you choose a state with a high population and regular natural disasters, the rate will be higher.

REAL ID

You may or may not have heard of the REAL ID Act, which was passed following 9/11 as an encouragement to states that they should be firmer with their rules surrounding driver's licenses. States are not required to comply, but a REAL ID will be required to enter airports and federal facilities by the end of 2020. If you ever want to set foot in such places, you are going to need one.

You will need a compliant driver's license for this, which will have a gold star in the corner. Alternatively, you can continue to use your passport when you travel domestically by air – but only if you have chosen a home state that has NOT complied with the REAL ID Act.

The problem here is that you have to be able to meet the associated proof of residency requirements, and that means you need something along the lines of a bank statement or credit card bill, which can be achieved through mail forwarding. You can also use a receipt from an RV park that shows you stayed for at least 30 consecutive days in the state. Research what will be required in your chosen home state – and whether it has complied with the READ ID Act – before making your selection.

Health Insurance

Not only will you need to purchase this in your chosen state of residence, you are also going to need to choose your plan very carefully. If using the Health Insurance Marketplace, you will need to select an option that doesn't penalize you too heavily for visiting an out of network medical facility. If you are retired and are still making use of an insurance plan provided by your previous employer, make sure that you will still be covered while you are out of that state. If you are on Medicare, you will need to notify them of your change of state residency to be sure that you are still covered.

You cannot open a bank account without a residential address due to the Patriot Act – and you can't use a mail forwarding address. However, you are allowed to use the residential address of a friend or family member and you won't usually need to provide any proof that you actually live there. It's worth asking that question before you make any plans – some banks will ask for a utility bill or other form of proof. It's also worth asking how they reinforce their residency requirements.

Once you have figured out how to secure the bank accounts you need, you should also check to see whether you're going to find your accounts easy to use. Can you bank online, for example? Do you need to visit a branch to deposit a check, or do they have an app for that? Do they have ATMs across the nation? You are going to need easy access to your money at all times, so you want to choose a bank that can help you make that happen.

Jury Duty

There is always the possibility that you will be called up for jury duty in your home state, and it's not always something you can get out of. Be sure to factor this possibility into your decision, as you could be required to head back to your home state at any time.

Voting

Every state has different rules when it comes to how you can register to vote and whether you need to be present to actually cast your vote. To make sure you can continue to exercise this vital democratic right, research the specifics for the home state you have in mind before making a selection.

Home Schooling

If you are a parent and plan to take your kids with you on the road, be sure to check the law in your chosen home state when it comes to home schooling. Some will require curriculum approval and will want your kid to be tested, others have no rules at all. Having to head back to your home state for tests can be a pain, so it's a good idea to check.

We mentioned earlier in this chapter that there are three states chosen above all others by RVers. If you're wondering why that is, let's take a quick look:

- Florida has no income or investment income and has a lot of choice when it comes to health insurance. Vehicle insurance is at the middle range and the location is pretty convenient if you plan to travel the east of the country. It also has mail forwarding companies to provide a street address.

- Texas has no state income tax either, and vehicle registration fees are low. However, there is an annual inspection (though it can be postponed until the next time you are back in the state). You can also renew your driver's license and register to vote by mail.

- South Dakota applies a four percent excise tax to vehicle purchases but has no other sales tax. It has no state income tax, reasonable vehicle registration fees and no state vehicle inspection. Vehicle insurance is particularly low and driver's licenses are also reasonable, though you'll have to appear in person to renew.

What About Your Pets?

Animal lovers often comment that they couldn't possibly switch over to a life on the road because they wouldn't be able to take their pets. Actually, that's not true – and as long as your animal has your RV as its home base and place of safety, it's likely that they will enjoy the new sights, sounds and especially smells just as much as you will.

But that doesn't mean you should just open the RV door for the dog and set off. Your pets are completely reliant on you for their every need and it's your responsibility to make sure they will be safe and healthy as they travel alongside you.

Make sure you've ticked every item off this list before you leave to be certain you've fulfilled that responsibility:

- Add an extra line to your budget for pet fees. A lot of campgrounds and RV parks will want you to pay a small extra amount if you're taking a pet with you (although this is more likely to be the case for dogs than cats). You will also need this budget line for other pet related costs, such as food, vet visits and medication if it needs any.

- Make sure your pet has all their vaccinations up to date and on record. Again, this is something you may well require to be allowed to have a pet with you in an RV park. If you are intending to cross the border, into Mexico or Canada, you are also going to need to be able to present a valid certificate showing that your animal is rabies free. You also want to make sure your best friend is healthy, of course, because you will be coming into contact with all sorts of unexpected adventures as you travel, so it's important that your pet is protected from catching any unpleasant illnesses. You will also want to make sure you have treated your pet for heartworm, ticks and fleas, all of which you may encounter along the way.

- Make sure you can find your pet if it happens to run away or get lost. This is particularly likely at first, because your pet will need to adjust to the new lifestyle just as much as you will. Invest in a sturdy collar that has your phone number and name on it so that anyone who finds it knows it's not a stray and how to get hold of you. It can also be extremely helpful to have a tracking chip implanted so that a vet can scan it to find your information and return your pet to you.

- Invest in a comfortable pet carrier that your animal can consider its own den inside your RV. Spend some time acclimatizing your pet to this den before you leave, so that it already associates the carrier with safety and considers it a place to sleep and rest. You will be able to use this carrier to keep your pet safe in certain situations, such as while driving (if necessary) and if you leave the RV without them for extended periods.

- Consider how your pet will live on a day to day basis. If you're taking a dog with you, make sure you have a decent leash with you for exercising, a long leash or chain for them to spend time outside the RV with you (a lot of campgrounds will require your dog be restrained at all times, while you certainly won't want it disappearing into the wilderness while you are boondocking) and that you have made sure to bear in mind its need for exercise when deciding where to stop for the night. If you are taking a cat, you may want it to stay inside for most of the time, but your RV will provide a lot less room for it to move around than your house once did. Make sure to bring toys, such as a laser pointer or a small cat tree, to keep it occupied. Consider also trying out a cat harness – some cats really enjoy going for walks in the same style as you would walk your dog, and this is a great way to solve the problem of taking an outdoor cat on the road that can't really spend time outside without you. Cats will also need a litter box, which you will need to find a secure place for in the RV.

Before you leave, it can be very helpful to take a weekend trip in your RV with your pet. Adapting to your new life may be overwhelming for your animal, if not downright traumatic. A weekend trip will familiarize your animal with its new situation and give you an opportunity to test out how well it copes and whether you will need to adjust your plans to include extra pet considerations before you move into the RV permanently.

RV Living On Your Own

You wouldn't be the first person to find themselves put off the idea of RV living because you don't have someone else to hit the road with. If this is a concern, you might feel reassured to know that most of your worries are probably based on your lack of experience (yet!) rather than the reality.

There's an obvious positive side to solo RV living: the freedom. You don't need to collaborate with anyone else on decision making, you can go exactly where you want to go, when you want to go there, and you can do whatever you choose once you arrive. You can even change your mind before you get there without disappointing your traveling partner.

If you are concerned about security, bear in mind that you are almost always either going to be in the company of a lot of other people or completely off the grid where there's nobody else at all. If someone breaks into your RV in a campground or RV park, slam down your fist on the horn and you'll attract a lot of attention pretty fast. At the other end of the scale, if you're out in the wilderness boondocking, there's unlikely to be anyone nearby to break in.

This doesn't mean you can't protect yourself, of course. It's always a good idea to carry such things as bear spray and some sort of weapon if you're going to places where there could be large wildlife on the prowl. But on the whole, you're no less secure in an RV than you are in a brick and mortar house.

What about loneliness? Again, you really do have to choose a solitary existence if you want to have one. At a campground, in a town or anywhere else man made, you're always going to find other people. It's not difficult to find someone to create a friendship with, wherever you may be. Look for a campfire, wander over and ask if you can join in – it's pretty uncommon that other RVers will say no.

You can also choose to connect specifically with people who are on the same journey you have chosen. Look for websites such as LonersOnWheels.com and RVSingles.org to find organizations that cater specifically to people who have chosen to hit the road alone. They will help you find and meet up with other people who share your mindset and keep in contact along the way. People who choose this lifestyle have formed a loose tribe across the nation and they will be more than willing to welcome you in.

Setting Up Your Budget

Even a nomadic lifestyle comes at a cost, albeit a much lower one than you were paying before. You no longer need to pay a mortgage and your utility costs will be a whole lot less in such a small space, but you'll be adding additional costs to your budget too, such as fuel.

The transition to your new life will go much more smoothly if you have a solid understanding of your financial needs. That way, you will know how long your savings will last and you will be confident of how much you need to earn on a weekly basis while you are traveling.

Take the time to figure out your budget, including both your day to day needs and any potential unexpected costs. You may need to think about how you will achieve some of these items; for example, if you will be using a Laundromat, what is the average cost in the areas you will be visiting?

Your budget should take into consideration:

- Food: Both for you and any children or animals who are traveling with you. Bear in mind your cooking facilities to figure out how much you will need to rely on pre-cooked food or eating in restaurants (though the less you have to do this, the better for your budget and health). Figure out how much you spend each week on food and how your eating patterns might change once you're on the road (especially without many kitchen cupboards to store groceries).

- Fuel: How much do you plan to travel in an average week and how long do you intend to spend in each place? If you hope to visit a different place every day, for example, you will need a lot more money in your fuel budget than if you intend to spend a month in each location.

- "Utilities": You are going to need propane, fresh water and tank fills to keep your home functional. Find out how much these will cost in the areas you will be visiting and how much your RV uses (if you don't know, try living in your RV for a week to see how long its supplies last while in use).

- Personal Hygiene: You will still need to launder your clothes and purchase soap, shampoo and other items. You will also need to budget for haircuts, new clothes and so on.

- Insurance: You are still going to need to stay up to date with your health, dental, life and vehicle insurance. Find out exactly how much each of these will be (some, particularly health insurance, may be different for a nomadic lifestyle). You may also want to continue paying into a retirement account.

- Membership Fees: Depending on what you want to do while traveling and where you want to go, you might want to join gyms, trail organizations, RV groups or get a pass for National Parks.

- Internet and Phone: Especially if you plan to work remotely on a computer, you are probably going to need internet service, likely through creating your own hot spot. Visit your cell provider to find out the costs of keeping cell service and internet while on the road. Consider shopping around – some providers will offer a great deal to get you to swap.

- RV Maintenance: Your RV is a vehicle, and a vehicle needs maintenance. Research the average cost of maintaining your vehicle regularly and consider keeping a sum of money in reserve in case of emergency breakdowns.

- Parking and Camping Fees: To figure out how much these will cost, plan an example route for a month and figure out where you would stop. It's a good idea to do this in a similar part of the country that you intend to actually visit, because costs can vary wildly from place to place. Add up the total cost of campground fees, National Forest fees, RV park fees and any others to see an average monthly cost for the trip you intend to take and the way you hope to live.

- Entertainment: The idea of RV living is to exist on a much lower budget than you are right now, but it's also to get out there and see the world. You sure aren't going to want to arrive at a new place and sit there in your vehicle looking at it out of the window. What kinds of things will you want to do when you get there? Do you prefer hikes or theater visits? Do you want to visit museums or dine on local cuisine? Your idea of sampling the local culture will be unique to your tastes, so consider the kinds of things you will want to do, how often you will want to do them and how much they are going to cost.

We mentioned in that list the idea of having an amount of cash stashed away for emergencies. Your RV breaking down isn't the only potential need you could have, so if possible you should have a nest egg sitting in your bank when you leave, untouched until you absolutely need it.

* * * * *

Before we continue, I have a small favor to ask:

Could you please take a minute of your time to write an honest review of the book?

Your reviews are what keeps me going. I read every single one of them, and would be **extremely thankful** if you choose to share your thoughts with me.

* * * * *

Firming Up Your Finances

First things first: you're going to need a place to put your money, and it needs to be a place where you can easily access it. If, until now, you have banked with your local institution, it may be time for a change. While you will still be able to use your bank card, sort out payments online and withdraw cash (usually with an associated fee), you won't be able to walk into a branch of your bank to access the services you need.

For this reason, you may want to consider one of the nationwide banks that have a physical presence in most states, or all of them. The three for which this is the case are JPMorgan Chase, Bank of America and Wells Fargo.

To choose between them, visit their websites and look for branches along the route you plan to travel. Is the bank you're interested in represented well in the areas you hope to spend time? If not, you probably want to pick another.

Now you have somewhere to put your money, you're going to need some money to put there. To cover the budget expenses you listed in the last chapter, you're going to need a monthly income.

Now you've set that budget, you know how much you need to earn. In the old days, that would have meant odd jobs, working in the fields and shifts at a local business, if they had room for you. Don't worry, if you still want to go that way, you can – all those things are still out there and plenty of people choose to follow seasonal work.

For instance, the U.S. Forest Service hires seasonally for such things as surveying, camp hosts and even logging and clearing brush to prevent fires. Campgrounds and other tourist attractions are much busier in the summer months and are often unable to find help locally because most people want full-time, year round jobs. Farms need help at planting and harvest time, too – there are plenty of seasonal jobs, if you look around to see what's available, and your lifestyle makes you the ideal candidate to take these positions.

It's also worth taking a look at your current job and asking yourself if it could be done from a remote location. Is there a need for you to be at your desk in the building every day? Could you get away with just swinging back through once a month for a meeting?

If you think there's a possibility, ask to speak with your boss. Offer a proposal, pointing out that you will still be able to complete your duties (and explaining how) while saving on the overhead expenses of office space. Once you've seen your budget, you may even be able to offer a pay cut while you're in the road, if you feel comfortable doing so.

You could also take a look at nationwide job listings for remote work – you might be surprised how many are available. Alternatively, become a freelancer in your area of expertise by performing contract jobs through a website such as Upwork.com or FieldAgent.net, on which you can bid for contracts and short term work.

This option works particularly well if you have a specialist skill that can be performed via the computer from any location, such as administrative tasks, bookkeeping and writing. You can also find specific websites for other job types, such as tutor.com for teachers or Bookeeper360.com for bookkeeping. On most of these sites you will need to build a reputation as a solid worker, usually by taking less-than-ideal contracts at first to gather positive reviews, but in the long term you should be able to find plenty of the kind of work you would be happy doing.

Another option is to become a vendor on Amazon or eBay, purchasing unique items and then selling them on again at a profit. This is a particularly good option if shopping is one of your preferred pastimes – your budget and living space might not stretch to allow you to buy all the things you would like for yourself, but purchasing to then sell could certainly scratch the itch!

As you can see, making a living on the road is nowhere near as tricky as it might seem at first. You can either concentrate on one of these avenues or mix and match; for example, in the summer you might work as a guide at a national monument, while in the winter you might work remotely completing contracts and search for part time shifts at bars and restaurants. Your options are almost as limitless as the destinations you can choose to visit!

Caring for your RV

Before you go anywhere, we cannot recommend highly enough that you take the time to become familiar with your own personal bible. No, not the religious kind – the vehicle version.

Your owner's manual is your new best friend, because it will tell you everything you need to know about taking care of your portable home. It will give you tips to take care of it on a regular basis and to fix things as and when they go wrong – which they absolutely will.

Your home is constantly on the move, which means it suffers stresses and strains that a normal house will never experience. Every bump in the road, every tight corner and every gravel path on the way into a campsite is a knock, a rattle and a shake that is causing something, somewhere to work itself a tiny bit looser than it once was.

You are going to want to put together a care kit before you leave, because there's no telling where you might be at the moment when something goes wrong. As well as maintenance tools and basic replacement parts for the vehicle end of things, you'll want glue and screws and other repair items for the cupboards, shelves and other parts of your home.

Your owner's manual will also give you a good idea of what kind of a maintenance schedule you'll need to plan. For example, every time you leave to move to a new destination, you'll want to check tow bars and tires, apply lubricant to moving parts and make sure the propane is turned off.

On a daily basis, you'll need to check battery, holding tank and propane levels and clean your solar panels. On a monthly basis, you'll want to check the generator oil and filter, test the CO2 and LP alarms, inspect and clean your vents and check the tire pressure. Annually, you'll need to inspect the roof, seals and seams and clean the slide out.

That's a basic list – yours may be different and there could be a number of other necessary items on it. Make sure you have created a check list for yourself and that you follow it religiously, no matter what happens, because the alternative is going to be repairs.

It's not a great alternative, largely because it's going to take big chunks out of your budget. RV repair shops are pretty expensive even just for hourly rates, let alone for the replacement parts you might need to purchase. Add to that the potential cost of having your RV towed from a remote location and you start to see how expensive it can get when things go wrong. But don't worry, you can prevent this from being a regular occurrence. The more you can do yourself, and the more care you give your vehicle to ensure it stays in good health, the lower the possibility that you're going to be faced with a nasty bill for repairs.

You might be thinking that you're simply not proficient at the kind of maintenance we're talking about and you'd much rather budget for repairs. This is a mistake. You can find all manner of guides to fixing and caring for your RV on YouTube and you'll soon discover that it's not nearly as frightening as prospect as you're imagining. In the end, you'll thank yourself for learning this new skill and saving yourself a whole lot of money and frustration in the process.

Safety on the Road

Four walls and a roof provide a great deal of safety, as does a familiar routine. On the road, there are a number of areas in which you will want to pay attention to your personal safety, both in terms of natural hazards and manmade.

These include:

Accidents

Driving an RV is absolutely not the same experience as driving any other vehicle you might be familiar with. Unlike cars, motorcycles and four wheelers, you are dealing with a large and ungainly home on wheels that doesn't always like to cooperate with an inexperienced operator.

The best way to mitigate any potential problems is to find a local RV driving class that will help you master the basics. This will cover everything from backing up in a vehicle that's 30 feet or longer, maneuvering through narrow city streets, weather driving and coping on the highway. If you can't find a local class, search for an educational DVD or online resource that will give you the information you need.

With or without a training class under your belt, make sure you take some time to practice driving your RV in a familiar area. Take it out to empty roads you know well and try backing up and turning in quiet areas so you can get to know your turning radius for left and right hand turns, backing into spots and parallel parking.

Get to know your braking speed – you will have bigger brakes than on a normal vehicle, but only because your RV weighs so much more. Learn the top speed your vehicle can go without strain so you are aware of how much time and distance you will need to merge, overtake and otherwise travel in traffic. Finally, learn your blind spots – there will be plenty, and this will make it tough to maneuver in ways you will only grow to realize once you have practiced.

You may also want to request a walk through at your dealership when you purchase your vehicle. Many will offer this service, in which they will show you everything from how to switch the headlights on to whether there is a remote for your slide out. Every model is different, so it can be very helpful if the dealer shows you exactly what quirks yours will have.

Finally, make sure to request a pre delivery inspection, which will involve an expert walking through your RV to check that everything is safe and in place. They will look for leaks, tire pressure, tank levels and much more on your behalf, which can be extra peace of mind as you set out.

You may find it reassuring to know that, as the driver or passenger in an RV, you actually have odds of dying in a vehicle accident of just a third that of traveling in a normal car. However, there is a flipside to this – you are also more likely to be the cause.

Inexperience is one of the major causes, so do be sure to look for that training course or an RV boot camp, which you can find through the internet happening all across the country. This inexperience can cause such dangers as badly calculating your turns, failing to predict your stopping distance and failing to see other vehicles due to your blind spots.

Other causes include speeding, driving while too tired and overloading your vehicle with too much weight. Failing to properly attach trailers or other vehicles, or even parts of the RV itself, can be a hazard. Keep these things in mind, because you are now in charge of operating a larger, more dangerous vehicle than you may ever have driven before. You are a hazard to others on the road, and you are also in charge of keeping your own home secure and safe between destinations.

Just as you would in a brick and mortar home, you will want to prevent harm from fire and leaks. RV fires are relatively common, so please do make sure you have smoke extinguishers at either end of the vehicle and one outside, too. Make sure to check your tires every time you leave a place and, if possible, purchase an RV that has two ways to escape in the event of a fire. Smoke detectors are vital and should be added to your list of things to check regularly. Finally, always – always! – turn off your propane takes before you drive.

Carbon monoxide poisoning is another concern you should be aware of. Make sure your propane system is checked regularly and be sure to learn the ins and outs of how it works from your manual so you can check it each time you travel. Again, make sure to have a carbon monoxide alarm fitted and avoid leaving your engine or generator running while you are asleep.

Symptoms of carbon monoxide poisoning include dizziness, nausea, confusion, weakness, headache, sleepiness and twitching muscles. If you experience these things, exit the vehicle immediately to access fresh air, shut down your generator and either call for help or take your vehicle to a professional – with the generator still shut down.

Safety From Wild Animals

Your non human neighbors can present you with plenty of challenges while you're on the road. While you're in more remote places, you of course run the risk of encountering wild wolves, bears and big cats. Make sure to carry bear spray and keep an eye on local websites for Game & Fish, the U.S. Forest Service or the National Park Service to see if predator activity has been reported in your local area.

To stay safe from bears, be cautious while outside your vehicle at night and try not to cook too close to your RV – store your food inside plastic to keep the scents sealed in. When moving around in the wilderness, make lots of noise – and if you come across a cub, be especially careful an exit the area swiftly, because the mother is almost certainly nearby and will be fierce in protecting her young.

To learn how to keep yourself safe in the wilderness, you may want to consider taking a hunter safety course before you boondock for the first time. Many states in which hunting is a popular pastime will offer this service; in some, it is mandatory before a person can purchase a hunting license. If you can't find any on offer at your starting location, look for one along your route. It's not hard to find them in the Midwest, though you may need to time your trip appropriately as most are offered prior to hunting season's open or before licenses go on sale.

Of course, predators are not the only animals to be aware of. A quick check on the internet and you'll find all sorts of stories about visitors to national parks who thought it was a good idea to pose for a selfie with or try to pet an elk or a bison and were punished for their ignorance. Do not approach wild animals – no matter how gentle or cute they look, always remember to respect the fact that they are not tame.

Snakes, spiders and lizards are also a concern on the road. Familiarize yourself before you leave with the species you may encounter on your route and how to apply first aid in the case of a bite. If you are bitten, try to take a picture of the creature that bit you and immediately call for help – it can often save your life to call for an ambulance rather than try to take yourself to the emergency room because the paramedics will bring equipment with them to start the process of administering to the bite.

If you are allergic to stings from wasps, bees or hornets, make sure to carry an epi pen with you in the RV at all times and to replace it when it runs out of date.

Even mosquitoes and ticks can be a big issue. These are not just pests, they are also carriers of potentially fatal diseases such as West Nile, Rocky Mountain Fever and

Lyme Disease. Check yourself for ticks regularly, carry mosquito spray to be used liberally during mosquito season and stay appraised of what diseases may be present in the local area through the region's public health system. You can usually find these entities on a website or social media.

As you travel across the nation, you are going to find out fast that weather systems can change on a dime – and the climate in each area is going to be different. You will encounter snow, rain, hail, wind, ice, lightning and other conditions that make is less safe to drive.

The National Weather Service has a website that will allow you to plan ahead, while you can also purchase weather radios that will alert you to any incoming dangerous systems. Plan your journey to avoid bad weather as much as possible, whether by taking a different route or delaying your departure. If you find yourself traveling in bad conditions, first and foremost you should slow down. Crawling along at five miles per hour may be frustrating, but it will save your life if you catch a patch of black ice and lose control. Always remember that your RV is not agile and will react in unwieldy ways.

Calling For Help

If you plan to travel between cities and stick mostly to RV parks and campgrounds, you are more likely to remain within cell signal range at all times. However, if you are planning to boondock or travel to states such as Wyoming, where there is a great deal of distance between towns, you may find yourself without a signal at least some of the time.

In terms of keeping up with your email, that's not really a problem – if you're boondocking, it's likely because you want the isolation. However, if something happens and you need to call an ambulance or the police, you are going to need to be able to do so no matter where you are.

There are items you can purchase to improve your chances of being able to call for help. A cell signal booster is going to be relatively expensive, but it can provide you with the ability to head into the wilderness in safety. A personal locator beacon will meanwhile send out a signal to the local search and rescue service via satellite in the case of a life threatening emergency.

Parking With Safety in Mind

There are certain tips you can bear in mind as you stop in a new place that could potentially save your life, whether you suddenly encounter a forest fire or you are targeted by a dangerous individual. The most important of these is to always park in such a way as to make it easy to leave in a hurry.

Do your turns and navigating before you stop rather than as you leave so that you are facing the exit and can simply turn on the engine and leave.

Meanwhile, be cautious of other people and don't open your door for strangers, especially if you are in an isolated place. You can give the impression of there being more people than just you in the RV by putting out additional chairs or footwear, which will deter anyone looking for an easy victim.

Even though you will always be in unfamiliar places, be sure to learn where you are and how to get back to a main road, whether in your RV or on foot. Consider investing in motion lights or a motion detector alarm, particularly if boondocking – these will let you know if someone or something has approached your vehicle without your knowledge.

You may also want to invest in secure latches for your windows and doors and a weapon to protect yourself if someone or something does get inside. Be aware that gun laws are different in every state, so you'll want to check into that before making the decision to invest in one. In most cases, you will need to carry your firearm unloaded, locked away and stored somewhere they are not visible from outside the vehicle, with the ammo kept elsewhere.

Finally, if possible, make sure someone is aware of your location or that you have installed a locator app on your phone so that you can be found if necessary.

Choosing Where to Stop

By now, you likely have a good idea of the states, places and towns you would like to build into your journey, but have you thought about the places you will want to stop at each of these destinations?

The style of RV you have chosen is going to affect what kind of place you can stop, as we alluded to in an earlier chapter, but by far the biggest factor in your decision is going to be personal choice. Let's take a closer look at each of your available options:

Camping

RV parks are available all across the nation – it will almost never prove difficult to find one along your route. They range from short term to long term and, as private businesses, will differ in cost and the amenities offered. There may even be entertainment available.

Do your research before you set out for a new destination because you will want to make sure spaces are available at the time of the season you are arriving; that the amenities you need are available; and whether you are happy with the price and/or can access a deal if you stay for a particular amount of time. Be aware that some RV parks require annual membership and are probably best avoided unless you'll be staying a very long time. Location is also important – if you're planning to explore the area on foot, you will want an RV park that's close to the action.

You can also choose to camp on National Forests, in state parks and in National Park Campgrounds. The advantage of this is the surroundings, which will place you smack bang in the middle of some of the most beautiful terrain your destination has to offer. Cost will vary according to location and time of the year and each campground will offer different amenities.

Be aware that some of these camping sites will only be
open at certain times of the year and will close down due
to weather – they may get snowed in or heavy rain may
make the gravel or dirt roads impassable. Some will be
exorbitant in cost at certain times during the season in
response to high levels of demand. You may also need to
book in advance and you will want to check for
restrictions on vehicle size and type, as well as for the
rules imposed on a particular camp site.

Boondocking

For a lot of RVers who choose the nomadic lifestyle, boondocking is the heart of their decision. This style of camping means to park up pretty much anywhere it's legal for a vehicle to be but that is in the wilds without access to amenities of any kind or the presence of other people.

The upsides of this style of camping include the freedom to enjoy incredible surrounds without the presence of other people and the fact that there's not usually an associated parking fee for you to pay. For many people, the idea of being alone in the beauty of nature is extremely enticing.

The downsides include, of course, a lack of access to amenities, which means you will need to bring your own water and power with you. You'll want a solar battery system that will charge throughout the day and large holding tanks for water and waste that can then be emptied and filled at a dump station. You are also isolated from help if needed, so you will want to make sure to pay close attention to the safety tips in the previous chapter.

The U.S. National Forest Service allows camping on its land outside of designated campgrounds. As with boondocking, you will be parking up without access to any amenities, including trash or toilets. However, it is free up to a certain time limit (usually just over two weeks) as long as you follow the rules imposed on that part of the forest. For example, in most places you will not be allowed to park on the road itself but must navigate into a pullout, and you will need to be at least a mile from a campground.

Local Forest Service offices will be able to guide you with maps and information about the roads and potential parking spots. They will also be able to appraise you of the rules you will need to follow.

Bureau of Land Management terrain is also usually free to camp on. BLM land covers up to a quarter of the nation and for the most part a fee is not charged to access it. You will usually be allowed to camp for up to 14 days and you can choose locations that are as isolated or close to a town or main road as you like. Check the BLM.gov website for further information on the areas you are heading to.

The BLM also has "Long Term Visitor Areas" that are very popular with nomads and have been developed with better roads and facilities. However, this investment means that a fee is charged to make use of the site. Visit a BLM office to pay this fee and get your permit.

Be aware when camping in this manner that both entities have a policy of Leave No Trace. Always make sure that you leave your campsite in exactly the manner you found it – or better – in order to preserve the beauty of these natural areas for the future.

When you are travelling long distances, you're probably going to want to stop overnight along the way. You may even find yourself planning a trip so you can spend one night in certain places for time to explore.

Most large retailers will be agreeable to your staying overnight in the parking lot (although, obviously, they will be less friendly if you set up shop for too much longer). Walmart, Cabela's and Target are known to be accommodating, as their parking lots generally sit unused overnight. Cracker Barrel is a favourite among nomads because they are particularly friendly in terms of allowing you to stay, size of spaces and well lit locations. Do try to make purchases with the business while you are there as a show of good faith.

Check with the manager before you stay, as some individual stores even in these chains will not want you to stay for certain reasons, such as city ordinances or overcrowding.

You can also park up in a city on a side street or in an industrial area, though check for signage that prohibits you from parking an RV in that place. However, there are often city ordinances that will allow an RV to be parked, but do not allow you to then sleep in that RV. This option is a last resort and one in which you will probably need to keep the lights off, make sure there are no signs of your presence and move on as soon as possible.

Rest areas are another option, though some will simply be pullouts along the road with no amenities and others may have stores, bathrooms or even dining areas. The latter is often an ideal place to pull over and spend the night, with access to supplies, food and other amenities while you are there. Be aware that each one will have its own rules and regulations as to how long you can stay, at what time you should leave and so on.

Truck stops are another option, but again each one will differ in terms of how welcome you are in an RV, where you should park and when you should leave. Be sure to make some purchases in the truck stop itself as a show of good faith. And do make sure not to take a spot needed by a trucker – they are mandated by law to rest along the way and must only do so at truck stops. Keep your slide outs closed and be mindful of others' needs while you stay.

In Summary

The information in this book was designed to give you an overview of the considerations you will need to bear in mind before you set off on an adventure like none you have ever experienced before. By the time you read these words, you should know if the idea of nomadic living makes you feel excited and eager to set out, or if it may not be for you after all.

If it's the former, there is nothing stopping you from getting out there right now in search of your new mobile home. It's time to let the world guide you along a treasure trail of experiences.

As you've probably gathered while reading this book, the only thing you can be certain of as you embark on an RV adventure is that your plans will have changed along the way. That doesn't mean you can't be extremely diligent in planning and researching everything from your camping destination to the jobs you will take as you travel – it just means you will need to be flexible.

Changed plans, a completely new lifestyle and letting go of everything you've ever known – this is a big step to take, there can be no doubt. But there is also no time like the present and nothing that's holding you back. If the RV life is for you, and you can't wait to get on the road and see what the world might have in store, then start your adventure right now – after all, what are you waiting for?

Special Thanks

I would like to give special thanks to all the readers from around the globe who chose to share their kind and encouraging words with me.

Knowing even just one person found this book helpful means the world to me.

If you've benefited from this book at all, I would be honored to have you share your thoughts on it, so that others would get something valuable out of this book as well.

Your reviews are the fuel for my writing soul, and I'd be **<u>forever grateful</u>** to see *your* review, too.

Thank you all!